MW00443955

4○
WEEKS

Also from Heather Doyle Fraser

Daily Gratitude and Intention Journal: An Abundant Life

40 Weeks: A Daily Journey of Inspiration and Abundance

HEATHER DOYLE FRASER

40
WEEKS

A Weekly Companion
Journal & Reflection Guide

Calliope House Press

Calliope House Press

Copyright © 2016 by Heather Doyle Fraser
www.beyondchangecoach.com

All rights reserved. No portion of this book may be
reproduced or copied in any form without written
permission from the publisher.

Published 2016

Copyeditors: Bridie O'Shaughnessy and Danielle Baird
Cover Design: Danielle Baird
Book Design: Danielle Baird
Photo Credit (author photo): Todd M. Rensi

Printed in the United States of America

ISBN–13: 978–0–6926–2735–8
ISBN–10: 0–692–62735–9

First Edition

Calliope House Press — Dublin, Ohio
www.CalliopeHousePress.com

*This book is dedicated to
my sister, Stephanie.*

TABLE OF CONTENTS

a time of
RELEASING

a time of
EMBRACING

INTRODUCTION

This weekly companion journal and reflection guide was originally written to accompany *40 Weeks: A Daily Journey of Inspiration and Abundance,* but it became so much more than that. It became a book unto itself.

Why 40 Weeks?

During the writing of the first book, I realized how pivotal the time period of 40 weeks (or nine months) is. It is exactly the time it could take to create a new life or a new way of being. This time period gives us space to transform or transmute what we currently experience in our daily lives into something more or something different.

I have realized that the transformations and changes that I have the privilege to witness regularly as a coach (and in my own life) follow patterns: a time of Opening, a time of Allowing, a time of Releasing, and a time of Embracing. And so, the book and this companion guide naturally fell into four parts or sections — one for each season of change and transformation. These parts are each comprised of ten weeks.

I created this companion because I wanted people to be able to journal and reflect upon their lives as they embark on their 40 week journey. When you have a guide and a formal place to put down all of your intentions, thoughts, feelings and emotions, and your commitments it is so much easier. It gives you a sense of forward movement and also clarity because you can see where you are in this moment, but then also where you were a week ago or two weeks ago or ten weeks ago. I wanted to create a safe place where everyone would be able to Open more, Allow more, Release more, and Embrace more, and I think this companion journal will help you to do that.

How to Use This Book

There is no right or wrong way to journal and reflect. You may move through this journal page-by-page in a very linear fashion. Alternately, you could go to a specific section if you want an entry that relates to the season in which you currently find yourself — Opening, Allowing, Releasing, or Embracing. Still another method would be to just randomly open the book and see what comes forth for you on that particular day. All of these options (and any others that you devise) will work to give you a touchstone or an anchor at the beginning of your day.

If you choose to move through the book in order, you'll find a series of prompts at the beginning of each section to help you "Set Your Intentions" for the forthcoming ten weeks.

Next, you will find four to seven writing prompts for each week based on the entries in the original book. You can complete these all at one go for a rather intense weekly experience, or complete one or two prompts a day here and there during the week. I recommend that you find the writing pace that feels best to you.

At the end of each ten week season, you will be asked to "Review and Reflect." With these exploratory questions, you will be asked to pause and acknowledge how far you have come and where you are now. This sets a foundation before moving forward into the next section.

My Hope for You

Whether you use this book in conjunction with *40 Weeks: A Daily Journey of Inspiration and Abundance* or on its own, I hope that this book brings you joy, comfort, and a sense of self-awareness and forward movement. I hope it is something you look forward to as part of your week. I hope this book gives a contented cadence to your days and allows you to set intentions and committed actions that serve your highest good. I hope that as you make your way through the journal you are able to see the shifts happening in your life more clearly, week after week, month after month.

a time of

OPENING

SET YOUR INTENTIONS

INTENTIONS**

Where in your life are you feeling the potential and possibility of an Opening right now? What could you do over the next few weeks to foster even more of an Opening here?

a time of OPENING

15

SET YOUR INTENTIONS

Where in your life are you feeling closed? How could you allow yourself to Open here, even in a small way? What could you do on a daily or weekly basis?

If the thought of Opening feels difficult or brings up feelings of fear or trepidation, that's okay. What would make it easier for you to consider the possibility and potential within and around you?

a time of OPENING

**SET YOUR
INTENTIONS**

How do you want to show up over the next ten weeks?
Set your intentions here and now.

a time of OPENING

WEEK 1

How can you make a fresh start today? What will you do differently to allow an opening for your personal growth and transformation?

What would you need to do and who would you need to be to inspire yourself?

Who surrounds you? Do you spend your time with people who fill you up, motivate, and inspire you or people who deplete you and convince you to stay small?

~ How do you feel when you are with them?

~ After you leave them?

WEEK 1

What inspires you?
What brings you joy?

Reflect upon what you want your day or week to look like:

~ Who do you want to be?

~ How do you need to show up in order to manifest your desires?

WEEK 2

What is your heart telling you today?
What would you like more of in your life?

a time of OPENING

What is holding you back? What could you do to release its hold on you and liberate yourself?

Reach inside your truth and look with fierce commitment at the person waiting. Examine the beauty, the sorrow, the strengths, and the uniqueness that is you. What do you see?

a time of OPENING

What would happen today if...

~ you could see the love in yourself?

~ you looked for the love in others?

~ you shared the love you experience with everyone you meet?

How are things beginning to shift for you? What are the subtle changes you have seen in yourself already?

WEEK 2

What is your commitment today? Be emboldened.

WEEK 3

What are you willing to take responsibility for in your life right now? If you were to take responsibility for everything — since you are capable of choosing how you react to people, places, and situations — how would that change things for you?

In what ways can you empower yourself today?

Where is the light for you at this moment in your life?

a time of OPENING

What mental path do you want to create or practice this week? How do you want to show up — in your thoughts, in your words, and in your actions?

How do you define success and failure?
What if you shifted your perspective around these concepts?
What if everything were just an opportunity to learn and grow?
How would this new understanding change things in your life?

a time of OPENING

Let your ideas around success and failure fall away and, just for today, look for the opportunities available to you.

~ What do you see?
~ What will you do differently?

40   40 WEEKS: A Weekly Companion Journal & Reflection Guide   ·   Heather Doyle Fraser

Take five long, deep, full breaths.

~ How do you feel when you focus on your breathing and allow yourself to come back to center?

~ What is possible from this place?

WEEK 4

We assign meaning to everything in our lives every day.

Today, reflect upon...

~ What is important?

~ What takes priority?

~ What is lovely?

~ What is challenging?

How will you consciously create your life today?
What will you do differently?

How can you push the boundaries of your comfort zone today and still stay in a place of ease?

List up to three things you can do to lean out of your comfort zone. What you will do to help you remember to stay in that place of ease?

a time of OPENING

Where do you see the harmony in your life? How can you be an active participant in creating this harmony?

What is your choice today? What is one small step you can make that will bring you more harmony and alignment?

WEEK 5

Who are you at a soul level?

What do you stand for? Can you see it in yourself?
Where does it come forth on a daily basis?

What are you an ambassador of at this place in your life? What do you want to bring to your life and the lives of others every day?

What discomfort are you willing to experience today to move you forward into growth and the life you want?

You have a choice in how you perceive yourself and your place in the world. What words will you use to describe yourself, your situation, and your circumstances?

Describe the magic you see and feel around you today. What miracles are happening right before your eyes: in nature, in the words of a friend or a child, in the actions of a stranger?

If you can't see the magic at first glance, take another look — focus on finding the magic.

What can you do to make your life easier today?

.

WEEK 6

How does love show up in your life?
How do you express your love to others and yourself?
What actions and words support this love?

We see what we want to see and what we expect to see every moment of every day. Why not set an expectation to see the best the world has to offer?

~ When you look around the moments of your life, what do you see?

~ What is your expectation?

Write down a little snippet of *The Story of You* today. Start where it feels easy. Create a story for yourself that speaks to your soul.

a time of OPENING

WEEK 6

Do something for yourself today that serves you fully. It can be as simple as showing yourself compassion and kindness when you most need it.

What will you do and why will it fill you up?

Be intentional about your choices. What will you choose to do today that you haven't done with purpose in the past?

a time of OPENING

Dance — just for one song. And when you are done, write about how you feel — in your heart, in your mind, in your body.

WEEK 7

How are you participating in your own transformation right now, in the past week, in the past month? What have you noticed as you have become an active participant in your life?

WEEK 7

What do you love? What fills you with purpose and passion?
Describe at least three ways you can honor what you love this week.

Who do you love? Describe at least three ways that you can honor the person or the people you love most this week.

Are the people, situations, circumstances, places, and possessions that surround you building you up and making you a better person, or are they tearing you down and keeping you from your best self?

What can you do to foster and nurture the best and most loving outcome for yourself?

What will you make of this day?

Do you feel fear or tension when faced with change or the unknown? How can you dance with that uncertainty today, and live in concert with it?

Have you given away your power to a person, a situation or an emotion without realizing it? Take it back now. Retrieve it with your heart.

Write the story here that allows you to take it back for yourself.

WEEK 8

Possibility, potential, and opportunity are waiting for you every day, every moment. Being open to seeing these gems is your job.

~ How can you flip your perspective today?

~ Where can you see your possibility?

WEEK 8

We create our abundant lives choice by choice and step by step.
What gives you purpose and meaning? What are you choosing?

Actively seek out and make choices to support the life
you envision for yourself. Describe what a week filled with
purposeful experiences would look like for you.

a time of OPENING

Take five deep breaths to settle and ground yourself.
Feel the breath fill your body and calm you.

Now, set a timer for two minutes and recite to yourself,
"I AM ENOUGH."

When you have finished, write about how you are feeling after
this experience. For instance,

~ How do you feel in your body?
~ Did this bring up anything unexpected?
~ Where are you opening to something new?

What would it look like if you were to choose love today? What would it be like if love were the foundation for your day?

What are you creating? Envision your highest goals and ideals and move toward that amazing reality one step at a time.

Start now with your intentions and committed actions.

WEEK 9

Take a short walk in nature. Allow yourself to be comforted by its beauty, its changes, its cycles, and its wonders.

Write about what this brings up for you in your heart and soul. What truth has been waiting to come forth?

Change... we can embrace it and act on the opportunities that arise or we can resist it and stay in the safety of sameness.

What are you choosing to do at this moment? How will this choice help you in the present moment and in the future?

What are you afraid of at this time in your life? Is there a way that you could flip that fear to a place of excitement?

Breathe. Open to the possibility of something different.

a time of OPENING

Your greatness is there within you waiting for your acknowledgement and action.

Your opportunity is now... where can you start planting and nourishing the seeds for your new creation?

What does it mean to be all of you today?

WEEK 10

What does it mean to you right now to open...

~ to your self?

~ to your body?

~ to your heart?

~ to your soul?

What blessings do you see around you? Describe what it feels like to notice their wonder and imperfections together.

Slow down and engage your senses. If you had to describe your most lovely day with all of your senses (sight, sound, smell, touch, and taste) what would the day look like? Describe all of its luscious abundance and see yourself in this picture.

What would you need to do to create this day now?

a time of OPENING

Explore your potential and possibility.

Are you ready for your next step? What will it be?

Where do you need to feel comforted today? Where are you longing for peace and rest?

You can give that gift to yourself.

a time of OPENING

WEEK 10

Make a deep connection with someone today. Be curious about what brings them joy and fulfillment and celebrate their greatness. Describe their reaction and how it feels to connect with someone in this way.

Be gentle and kind with yourself as you continue to live with purposeful intention and focused action.

What can you do to show yourself the loving kindness you would show to a child, a dear friend, a partner, or a beloved animal?

REVIEW & REFLECT

Before you answer these reflection questions, go back to pages 14–19 and review the intentions you set for *a time of Opening*.

Where in your life have you felt the potential and possibility of an Opening during the last ten weeks? What have you done differently during this time to foster change and transformation?

REFLECT

Celebrate and acknowledge how far you have come and all you
have accomplished in this area.

Are there any places in your life where you are still feeling particularly closed at this time? How can you allow an opening in these areas, even in a small way?

REFLECT

As you move into the time of Allowing, look for places where the intersection of the seasons in this journey (Opening, Allowing, Releasing, and Embracing) come together to create a fullness in your growth and transformation.

a time of OPENING

a time of

ALLOWING

SET YOUR INTENTIONS

Where in your life are you feeling the potential and possibility of Allowing right now? What could you do over the next few weeks to foster even more Allowing there?

Where in your life are you feeling the need to control at this time? How could you bring a sense of Allowing here, even in a small way? What could you do on a daily or weekly basis?

If the thought of Allowing feels difficult or brings up feelings of fear or trepidation, that's okay. What would make it easier to consider the idea of letting go of some of this external control?

**SET YOUR
INTENTIONS**

How do you want to show up over the next ten weeks?
Set your intentions here and now.

WEEK 11

How do you intend to spend your time today? Is it in the service of the people and values that make you whole?

Who are the people that surround you on a regular basis?

~ Do they fill you and lift you up?
~ Do they hold space for you to see possibility and potential?
~ Do they inspire you to be the best version of yourself?

WEEK 11

Take time to connect with someone who inspires you.

Notice how intentional connection with someone magical feels in your body and heart. Describe how you feel when you are around them. What are you inspired to do after being with them?

What are your morning rituals? How do they help to ground you and prepare you for your day?

Gratitude: that's a practice worth cultivating.

This week, use this page to write down three things for which you are grateful for every day and why.

What is happening in your body today? Are you feeling tension or discomfort, or are you acknowledging the overall strength and flexibility of your body?

Notice where you fall on the continuum, breathe into all of your splendor. Allow whatever comes up and savor the physical feelings and emotions that surface. Describe your experience.

a time of ALLOWING

Allow...
Surrender...
Release...

When you read these three words, what feelings and emotions come up for you? Why are these feelings and emotions just what you need at this moment?

WEEK 12

Whisper your secret longings and big dreams to yourself and write them down. You are safe.

WEEK 12

What would your day look like if you made a commitment to release your control of others and the situations in which you find yourself?

What if your focus shifted inwards towards your responses and reactions?

What if the abundance you imagine as part of your future is already here and you just aren't seeing it?

What if the contentment and well-being you are looking for are small AND sitting alongside the chaos of your daily experience?

a time of ALLOWING

WEEK 12

What if you looked for joy and abundance today — however small — and focused on the beauty of that smallness?

Imagine what your days would look like if your attention and focus allowed peace, contentment, and joy to grow even amidst chaos and uncertainty.

How can you be a gentle yet persistent voice in an area of your life that needs your attention?

WEEK 12

Describe what it would be like if you could access joy and abundance every day. Paint a picture with your words — don't leave anything out.

WEEK 13

What if acknowledging the greatness and the gifts within you was the first step to releasing the illusion of perfection?

What would you be free to create... to be... to do... after that first step?

Your joy rests in your greatness and your strengths.

What if that acknowledgement alone gave you permission to stop focusing on the outcomes and instead focus on the creation, the process, and the practice of your life?

What small things could you do differently with this shift in perspective?

Shift your perspective on a problem or challenge that has been frustrating to you. How can you view this difficulty as a place of learning, as an adventure, or as something you need to move forward?

a time of ALLOWING

Everything has a purpose.

Where in your life is something growing and flourishing, but you haven't recognized it until now?

Create a doodle or a picture here of what a good day looks like —
it can be abstract or literal. It can just be shapes or color. It just
needs to have meaning for you.

What are you feeling today? *(frenzied, calm, peaceful, contented, joyful, confused, busy, disappointed, sad, strong, accomplished)*

There is no wrong answer. Own your feelings and emotions and do not allow others to dictate them.

WEEK 14

Create an adventure for yourself this week. It can be big or small. How can you play in the vibrancy of your life... just for this moment?

What if you brought the attitude of a beginner — of wonder and newness — to each interaction, each observation, each breath today?

What would be different?

What would you need to do to step out of your comfort zone at this moment? Where is your resistance?

What does it mean to fully be you?

What would it feel like to inhabit a place where everything — all of your best parts and all of the parts you don't like so much — are all perfectly imperfect?

What if you dropped your badge of busy-ness?

What if you allowed yourself to be intentional today about bringing the FUN?

a time of ALLOWING

WEEK 14

Describe your version of spreading the light. Will you whisper it in quiet moments or give loud declarations or even do both? How will you allow your light to come forth?

a time of ALLOWING

WEEK 15

Be present and mindful.

Where is your joy today?

Check in with yourself.

~ What brings you a sense of calm?
~ What leaves you feeling agitated or frustrated?

How can you bring a sense of contentment to your life on a regular basis? Let's do more of that.

It's time for another dose of gratitude. Think of three things—people, activities, experiences, knowings for which you are grateful in this moment.

Write them down and allow them to sink in to your heart and soul.

a time of ALLOWING

What are your intentions for this week? Allow yourself to be grounded in your purpose. What will you commit to in order to bring those intentions to life? How will you make them happen?

Be gentle and kind with yourself. How can you create the space you need in your life to realize your intentions and dreams?

a time of ALLOWING

WEEK 16

If you allow yourself to become quiet and still, what knowledge opens up for you? Where do you feel a sense of waiting, unfolding, growing, or becoming?

WEEK 16

What would it look like if all of your boundless creative power came through?

When you look on yourself with loving kindness and self-compassion, what comes up for you? How can you gently hold your missteps and all of your strengths and gifts together?

WEEK 16

Today can be whatever you want it to be. What is calling to you right now? What is your vision for this day, this week?

Shine your light for all to see. Allow the dimness of doubt to slip away into the shadows. What does it look like to gently come back to your heart-centered self?

WEEK 17

Things can become complicated quickly... but what if today were easy?

What would that look like and feel like? Stop and imagine yourself moving through your day with ease and energy. See yourself flowing from one conversation to the next and one situation or circumstance to the next. Describe what unfolds here.

WEEK 17

What if you treated each moment with reverence? What if you made the cuddle on the couch or the act of walking outside to get your mail important?

What would change for you?

"STOP ACTING SO SMALL. YOU ARE THE UNIVERSE IN ECSTATIC MOTION."

— Rumi

What does this quote mean for you in this moment?

Be you. All of you.

Where will you allow a feeling or an emotion that has been difficult in the past for you? How will this allowing help you to more fully be in alignment with your highest self?

Look for the duality of lightness and heaviness as they exist in the same space. Where is the beauty in these two opposites together? How does each enhance the other?

WEEK 17

We all crave balance. And sometimes that doesn't feel easy.

If you feel out of balance, take a look at where you are spending your time and with whom. Are these activities and people in alignment with what you value? What choices can you make to support yourself today?

WEEK 18

Breathe into any uncertainty, doubt, or fear. Let these emotions come up. Look at them in the face.

How can you allow these emotions to pass through and still stay grounded in the present moment?

WEEK 18

Where can you take back your power today?
It's right here with your next breath.

Stop. Breathe. In this quiet moment, ask yourself what you can do right NOW to bring yourself more joy, calm or just a little relief.

What actions will you take to bring about this shift?

a time of ALLOWING

WEEK 18

We don't always look at how far we've come. What are you celebrating today?

Let this celebration motivate you to take that next step forward.

Notice the beauty and abundance around you. Describe it here.

Who can you send love and compassion to so that they may be able to see the world through your eyes?

a time of ALLOWING

WEEK 19

What patterns are you reinforcing? Some may serve you and some may not. If there are patterns that are not serving you, do something about it.

One small change can bring a huge shift. It can stop a pattern in its tracks and begin to build a new one. Where is your change today?

a time of ALLOWING

WEEK 19

Sometimes we need a dance break. Move your body — even for one song —and see what happens. Allow an unraveling and let your heart lead.

Pay attention. How are you feeling in your body before you dance? What happens when you are dancing? And finally, how do you feel afterwards?

How can you support yourself today?
Ask yourself, "What do I need to do right now?"

a time of ALLOWING

WEEK 19

Where can you bend to make things easier for yourself and others?

Where can you allow yourself to give and receive without care or reservation?

WEEK 20

Be intentional. Slow down. Fixate your attention on something mundane and ordinary.

What do you hear and see that you never noticed before today? Observe how it feels to be purposeful.

WEEK 20

Give yourself a gift today of 15 minutes of quiet without distractions — no phone, no media, no doing. What does it feel like to be still?

Where is your peace and calm today?
Where do you feel simple, whole, and free?

Allow your intuitive wisdom to take over your multi-tasking hands and mind.

Notice how it feels in your body and heart to live in the present moment.

Use your body wisdom as a compass to navigate your day.

Where do you need to take action or slow down?

REVIEW & REFLECT

Before you answer these reflection questions, go back to pages 102–107 and review the intentions you set for *a time of Allowing*.

Where in your life have you felt the potential and possibility of an Allowing during the last ten weeks? What have you done differently during this time to foster change and transformation?

REFLECT

Celebrate and acknowledge how far you have come and all you have accomplished in this area.

Are there any places in your life where you are still feeling the need to control at this time? How can you allow yourself to let go, even in a small way?

a time of ALLOWING

REFLECT

As you move into the time of Releasing, look for places where the intersection of the seasons in this journey (Opening, Allowing, Releasing, and Embracing) come together to create a fullness in your growth and transformation.

a time of

RELEASING

SET YOUR
INTENTIONS

Where in your life are you feeling the potential and possibility of Releasing right now? What could you do over the next few weeks to foster even more release here?

**SET YOUR
INTENTIONS**

Where in your life are you feeling the need to control and keep patterns, habits, and actions as they are even if they are not serving you at this time?

How could you bring a sense of Release here, even in a small way? What could you do on a daily or weekly basis?

If the thought of Releasing feels difficult or brings up feelings of fear or trepidation, that's okay. What would make it easier to consider the idea of Releasing that which no longer serves you?

a time of RELEASING

**SET YOUR
INTENTIONS**

How do you want to show up over the next ten weeks?
Set your intentions here and now.

WEEK 21

When we feel pain we often push it away, but what would happen if we embraced it instead and held it in our hearts as we would a small child?

When the pain has served its purpose, you can release it. What will you embrace today so you may release it tomorrow?

a time of RELEASING

You are ready for the next step. What will it be?

Change is all around us in every moment. What happens when you lean in to the change rather than resist it?

What if you accepted change as a natural part of your existence and allowed yourself to bend and shift as needed?

Start something you have been resisting or delaying.

No more excuses: what is the first committed action you need to take today?

What does stillness sound like and feel like to you?

a time of RELEASING

WEEK 21

What stories do you want to create around your abundance, power, and prosperity?

Transformation requires movement out of your comfort zone
and into possibility and potential. Where is your potential today?

WEEK 22

What do you need to do to release yourself from the shackles of the ordinary?

Choice is powerful.

What course of action are you choosing today?

Today, focus on just one thing — the committed, right action you need to take in order to move forward.

What is your next step?

Stop. Breathe. Ask the question, "What can I do to make things easier for myself today?"

Start there, with that very first thought and allow what comes forth as you tune in to your inner wisdom.

WEEK 23

Your body is a compass — listen to and honor its wisdom.
What is it telling you today?

Imagine a day where you feel joy, excitement, fulfillment and accomplishment, and every emotion that will serve you.

Describe that beautiful day here. Put down all of the details.

What can you do today to bring yourself more ease?
What can you do to create the day that lives in your imagination?

What will you do to make someone else's life easier today?

If joy and abundance were a part of your every day, how would that change you? What would you do differently right now?

a time of RELEASING

WEEK 24

Today, make space to be still and honor all of the changes you are making. Reflect on these changes and how you will nurture yourself this week to foster more forward movement.

WEEK 24

Listen to your heart in the stillness you create...
What is your next right action?

You can create what you desire. Where is your possibility and potential this week?

Bring the laughter. Bring the joy.

What shifts do you notice in your life when you allow the joy to come and stay with you — even for a few moments?

Your perception, your focus, your intentions, and your actions define your reality.

What will you make of today and this week? What will you choose? What will you do?

a time of RELEASING

What would change if you gave yourself permission to believe in yourself?

WEEK 25

What does freedom mean to you on a personal level?

WEEK 25

Sometimes our comfort zone is just where we need to be. And other times we need to stretch out of the safety of sameness and into possibility.

What will you stretch into today?

What values most define you at this moment in your life? What is important to you?

Declare yourself right here, right now. Commit to being the ambassador that lives within you. How will you show up today?

What if you looked for opportunity, possibility, and potential today instead of looking for ways that your day might be challenging or difficult?

What if you opened your mind to the possibility of receiving?

What would your life be like if you didn't engage with self-judgment or criticism?

For every unkind or judgmental thought you are experiencing — write it down and then write down a kind and loving replacement.

a time of RELEASING

WEEK 26

Where are you feeling and allowing a sense of hope right now?

Strength lives in your vulnerability. How will you embrace that truth today?

What do you need to release in order to heal?

We are all connected.

Where are you feeling connection in your world?

a time of RELEASING

Embrace your mistakes and missteps. They come to you for
a reason.

Where can you learn from them and and then start fresh, like a
morning breaking out of the dark?

Have you ever watched a sunrise? Every sunrise starts in the darkness. And then, it ushers in a new day without apology, without explanation. It becomes beauty every day.

How will you become beauty today?

a time of RELEASING

WEEK 26

What do you need to do this week in order to feel free?

WEEK 27

When was the last time you ran in the grass barefoot or danced in the rain?

It's time to nourish your senses. Do something today that makes you feel the joy of a child and then write down your experience here.

Allow yourself to feel a full range of emotions. What is coming up for you? Search out what you need and release what isn't serving you.

What would it feel like to soar untethered to a place where you are gleaming and supple?

Picture this place. Paint every detail on your heart and in your mind. Describe what feelings and visions come to you when you allow yourself to soar.

a time of RELEASING

What would be the best way to hold yourself in loving kindness today? What do you need from yourself?

WEEK 28

Start today with a practice of gratitude. What three things are you most thankful for today and why? Your list doesn't have to be beautiful and tidy. It can be messy and strange, too.

WEEK 28

When you are in a place of gratitude, your intentions are bigger, more expansive, more hopeful. What are your intentions for this week? How do you want to see your week unfold?

What is your commitment to yourself this week?

"WHAT WE CALL THE BEGINNING
IS OFTEN THE END.

AND TO MAKE AN END IS TO MAKE
A BEGINNING. THE END IS WHERE
WE START FROM."

—T.S. Eliot

What are you ending or releasing this week so that you can begin
anew next week?

How can you be more compassionate to yourself today?

a time of RELEASING

WEEK 28

Where is your edge at this moment? Where does your comfort zone stop and your growth zone begin?

What is one small step you can take to propel yourself forward?

WEEK 29

Acknowledge your greatness and celebrate what you see in your life.

Where is your purpose, your passion, your joy?

What would happen if you brought it into everything you do and each decision you make, even if it is small right now?

What would you like to create this week in your life?

Sometimes difficulties and challenges arise in life. But what would happen if you greeted the difficult times with appreciation?

Imagine what possibilities would open up if you said in the face of adversity, "Thank you. This is just what I need."

Anger or resentment — whether it is directed at yourself or another — is a mask for the fear or pain that sits just beneath the surface. Sometimes it seems less painful to be angry or resentful than it does to feel our own suffering.

Where do you need to send love and compassion today, this week?

WEEK 30

If you were asked to tell at least three people how much you appreciate them in your life and why, who would you talk to and what would you say to them? Be specific and get personal.

WEEK 30

Rewire your brain for joy this week, this moment —
What does it feel like to see the beauty around you and
acknowledge it fully with your body, your mind, and your soul?

Be BOLD.

Do something that stretches you. If mistakes are okay, if you do not have the pressure of perfection, what journey would you embark on right now?

WEEK 30

What if you acted as if you were already where you need to be at this moment in your life?

What would you accomplish if you released your expectations and enjoyed the process?

There will be a time when everything suddenly becomes clear, and your armor is no longer necessary.

What would it feel like to release yourself from your small ideas? What would it feel like to embrace your power and embody your joy?

REVIEW & REFLECT

Before you answer these reflection questions, go back to pages 186–191 and review the intentions you set for *a time of Releasing*.

Where in your life have you felt the potential and possibility
of a Releasing during the last ten weeks? What have you done
differently during this time to foster change and transformation?

REFLECT

Celebrate and acknowledge how far you have come and all you have accomplished in this area.

Are there any places in your life where you are still feeling the need to keep patterns, habits, and actions as they are even if they are not serving you at this time? What can you do to explore these places?

REFLECT

As you move into a time of Embracing, look for places where the intersection of the seasons in this journey (Opening, Allowing, Releasing, and Embracing) come together to create a fullness in your growth and transformation.

a time of

EMBRACING

SET YOUR INTENTIONS

Where in your life are you feeling the potential and possibility of Embracing right now? What could you do over the next few weeks to foster even more Embracing here?

Where in your life are you feeling yourself push away or doubt what you know in your heart will serve you? How could you Embrace that uncertainty even in a small way? What could you do on a daily or weekly basis?

If you are having difficulty imagining Embracing what lies before you and around you — or if the thought of stepping into this uncertainty in such a powerful way brings up feelings of fear or trepidation — that's okay. What would make it easier?

a time of EMBRACING

**SET YOUR
INTENTIONS**

How do you want to show up over the next ten weeks?
Set your intentions for the next ten weeks here and now.

a time of EMBRACING

WEEK 31

What is your truth — just in this moment?

Share yourself and your truth. People will show up differently because you are willing to declare yourself.

Transformation and growth require committed action.

What intention are you willing to commit to and act upon today?
What's your first step?

Observe how you view situations in your life — with abundance and hope or with a sense lack and unease?

If the future is not determined today, why not choose to move towards the best possible outcome? What can you do right now to move towards abundance and hope?

a time of EMBRACING

Is there a pattern in your life that no longer serves you? What if you replaced it with something that makes your heart sing?

What if you nurtured yourself with loving kindness in a way that you haven't before? What can you try this week that is new for you?

What if there were more kindness? What if every day you asked how you could be kinder to yourself and to others?

What would that look like today and this week?

Settle in to the stillness.

Reflect on your purposeful and mindful actions and words —
your commitments. How are they making a difference in your life?

What could you do to make more of an impact?

WEEK 32

Comfort yourself. Talk to the child that still exists inside of you. What does that pure and hopeful soul wish for you? What would that child do in your world today, this week, this month?

What if everything in your life was already a perfect fit?
What if you felt balanced?

What would these changes shift in you?

I am enough just as I am. I love myself unconditionally as I would love a small child who is unsullied with the worries of the world.

What do these words bring up for you in your heart and your soul?

The choice you make today doesn't need to be the last decision you make. Today's decision can be for your highest good in this present moment.

Create an intention for yourself right now. Make a sacred choice and it will lead you to the best right action in the next moment.

What would an adventure into the unknown look like for you right now, in this moment?

a time of EMBRACING

"DROP THE IDEA OF BECOMING SOMEONE, BECAUSE YOU ARE ALREADY A MASTERPIECE. YOU CANNOT BE IMPROVED. YOU HAVE ONLY TO COME TO IT, TO KNOW IT, TO REALIZE IT."

— Osho

Describe the masterpiece that is you.

a time of EMBRACING

WEEK 33

Where there is learning, there is no failure — it all serves a purpose.

What would you try if failure didn't exist?

Breathe.

Feel the sun on your face.
Truly taste your food.
Smile with loving kindness when people pass.

What you are feeling right now — whether joy or pain or
somewhere in between — is all life. How will you embrace it?

What if the sweet and the sad are poured out of the same vessel?

How will you say yes to both? What would it look like to surrender and continue to move forward with deep compassion for yourself and others?

What would you accomplish if you did not internalize the negative stories people tell you? How would your feelings, goals, and actions shift?

Rewrite your personal stories. Only you can put a limit on how far you will walk on your path.

What do you believe in right now?

a time of EMBRACING

What do you hold dear? What is important to you?
What do you expect to see unfold around you in your life today?

Sit with these questions in the quiet of your heart and listen.
Let your inner wisdom propel you forward and illuminate your
next steps.

WEEK 34

Create the day you envision as your highest self.

Draw or doodle a masterpiece of this dazzling beauty here.

What if you chose to experience today without judgment?
No judgment of yourself or others. No inner critic chattering
away providing seemingly endless commentary.

What would that look like? How would you feel?

What if we replaced criticism with simple observation? What if we replaced judgment with compassion?

Take three judgmental statements and replace them with simple observations or compassionate responses.

a time of EMBRACING

Perfection is an illusion.

Today, begin to release perfection and all the ways it shows up in your life. Take action even if you think you're not ready — even if you harbor the thought that you just might not be good enough.

What's your first step?

Happiness lives in the present moment. Today, this moment,
is just what you need. Breathe and notice how you feel. Let the
fullness of your experience gently embrace you.

a time of EMBRACING

WEEK 35

What if the thing you are most dreading this week is actually part of your journey and part of the adventure?

Describe how this shift in perspective could change your outlook, your thoughts, your actions.

We are all writing the story of our lives, one breath at a time.

See yourself today for the writer you are. What story would be the best one to tell today, this week? Focus on how you want to feel and then bring that into your life.

Sometimes we need a challenge or an adventure. Sometimes to get to the luscious essence of life we need to experience the uncertain path.

What does the uncertain path look like for you right now? What would you need to believe in order to take the first step down that path?

Slow down and give your day some love.

Where do you need it most right now?

We create our days and our lives — our realities. We choose how we respond — to the people with whom we interact and to the experiences in which we find ourselves.

What reality do you choose to create today?

a time of EMBRACING

WEEK 36

Where is your light this week? Look for it and you will find it. Allow the shadow to be there, and still, step into the light.

What do you think that experience — to look for and step into the light amidst the darkness — would feel like?

When you look inside to the depths of your heart and soul, what do you see?

We inspire others to do things they wouldn't have done without our support and encouragement.

But what if you supported yourself in that way, too? What if you set yourself up for success by showing yourself kindness and compassion? What would you be inspired to do?

How do you feel around the people you interact with on a daily basis? Do you feel uplifted... better for the time you spent with them?

Pay attention. With whom would you like to spend more time and why?

What brings you peace and contentment? How can you incorporate more of this in your life?

How do you start your day? Do you ease into it with intention or jump in and start swimming in the chaos and action already waiting for you?

A morning ritual is a wonderful way to set the pace of your day...

Pick something to try this week and describe here how things changed for you or how you felt different.

WEEK 37

What do you do every day? What has become a habit or a pattern for you? Do you love the patterns in your life? Do they serve you and set you up for success?

Take a look. List the habits and patterns that serve you and why. Then list some habits that you might want to change or replace.

Where have you experienced a learning in the past few weeks or months? How can you pull this learning forward into your present and future to help set yourself up for success as you move into your next adventure?

Sometimes consistency seems boring, and sometimes consistency can be beautiful and easy. Where can you incorporate more consistency in your life so that it feels beautiful and easy?

a time of EMBRACING

Where can you start something new this week?
Where have you been hesitating?

Write yourself a love letter.

Talk to yourself with that soft and caring voice you reserve for your beloved. Witness and acknowledge your accomplishments and describe the beauty within.

a time of EMBRACING

WEEK 38

What does the light inside of you look like?

WEEK 38

Embrace yourself with your words and actions this week.
Embrace yourself when you are feeling stunning and strong and
when you are feeling like you are not up for a challenge.

What does embracing yourself look like and feel like to you?

Sometimes... patience.

It could be the most potent and generous kindness you extend to yourself.

Where do you need to be more patient with yourself this week?

What are you ready to receive in this moment, in this season of embracing?

What would you need to do this week to embrace your soul's purpose?

What would bring your best day? What would bring you a sense of luscious fullness?

What would it look like to just be you right now, all of you?

WEEK 39

Your job this week: Create the space you need to expand into the corners of your life.

What does that mean for you? What will you need to do?

Today, inhabit all of the moods of your life without apology. Experience all of your emotions.

When you embrace yourself in this way, when you allow whatever is present to come forth, what does your inner wisdom tell you?

What do you need to do to create a life that nourishes and feeds your soul?

Abundance is all around us.

Allow your heart to open to the possibility before you. Where will you embrace the pleasure of receiving?

What would your future self ask of you today?

WEEK 40

What would bring you pleasure today?

There is remembering in pleasure. Whatever you learn with pleasure will imprint itself onto your heart and into your existence. Create a memory of pleasure.

What do you want to create in the coming months? Where is your next area of learning and growth? Where is your next adventure?

Where are you feeling resistance? Where are you feeling ease?

Growth and transformation can feel exciting and unexpected and challenging and simple all at once. Look for the crossroads of your wisdom and spend some time there.

a time of EMBRACING

What happens in your world when things get messy?
What happens when the vibrant colors of our lives run together
and become muddy?

"AS I EXPAND IN ABUNDANCE, LOVE, AND SUCCESS, I INSPIRE OTHERS TO DO THE SAME."

— Gay Hendricks

What does this quote mean to you now, in this moment? What does it mean for you as you embrace the next season of your life?

a time of EMBRACING

This day is just what you need, with all its imperfections and beauty and challenges and ease.

How will you be a participant in the growth and transformation waiting quietly to come forth, this day, this week?

Welcome the duality of our existence here in this physical world. Acknowledge and embrace all that comes to you for your highest purpose.

Give and receive freely for those you love, for yourself... for everyone.

REVIEW & REFLECT

Before you answer these reflection questions, go back to pages 268–273 and review the intentions you set for *a time of Embracing*.

Where in your life have you Embraced potential and possibility during the last ten weeks? What have you done differently during this time to foster change and transformation?

REFLECT

Celebrate and acknowledge how far you have come and all you have accomplished in this area.

Are there any places in your life where you are still pushing away what you know will serve you? How could you Embrace that uncertainty even in a small way?

a time of EMBRACING

REFLECT

As you move into the next season of growth and transformation in your life, let the process begin again naturally as you move forward. Look for places where the intersection of the seasons in your next journey (Opening, Allowing, Releasing, and Embracing) come together to create a fullness in your life.

a time of EMBRACING

ACKNOWLEDGMENTS

This journal and reflection guide was born out of my book, *40 Weeks: A Daily Journey of Inspiration and Abundance.* I would like to thank the readers of that book, who inspired me to write this companion whether they realized it or not. Thank you for sitting with me in spirit as I wrote this book.

I would also like to thank my husband Chris and my daughter Eva for supporting me through another book writing process. Your support means everything to me.

And thank you, Danielle Baird, for once again bringing my words to life with a beautiful design. I value your friendship and your expertise.

Acknowledgments

"This is my story.

I bring joy and transformation.
I shift perspectives and perceptions.
I explore possibility, potential, and opportunity.

I am willing to dig deep in my own life so
that I can help my clients achieve the same
transformation and abundance."

—Heather Doyle Fraser

ABOUT THE AUTHOR

HEATHER DOYLE FRASER is a Coach, Writer, and Creative Development Editor. As a coach, Heather works with individuals and groups — some of whom are writing their own books — who are seeking more joy, transformation, and ease in their lives. She holds the space for her clients as they find their authentic voice, move toward and acknowledge their inherent greatness, and achieve their goals and vision for an extraordinary life. When she is not coaching or writing, Heather enjoys making art, singing in her celtic band, The Ladies of Longford, and spending time in nature. Heather lives in Ohio with her husband and daughter.

If you would like to learn more about coaching or contact Heather, please visit her website at **www.BeyondChangeCoach.com**.

HEATHER DOYLE FRASER

40
WEEKS

A Daily Journey of
Inspiration and Abundance

What if you had the ability to focus on what's important, reflect on what matters to you, and appreciate the beauty, joy, and abundance around you every day? *40 Weeks: A Daily Journey of Inspiration and Abundance* will allow you to strengthen these abilities — one day at a time.

Here, you will find a daily companion — a touchstone — to bring you back to your inspired self and guide you through the stages of a transforming life. As you read and reflect on each entry, you will begin to notice yourself Opening, Allowing, Releasing, and Embracing as you experience each new season of becoming. In this book you will find:

- Active declarations for living a purpose and passion-filled life.

- Poetry.

- Quotes that speak to the heart.

- A place of loving kindness where you feel whole with both your greatness and your imperfections.

It's time to start your daily journey of inspiration and abundance.

Available on amazon.com and CalliopeHousePress.com